KINDERKIRK TEACHER BOOK

Birds

Words by Dean Morris

Raintree Childrens Books
Milwaukee • Toronto • Melbourne • London

Library of Congress Number: 77-8302

1 2 3 4 5 6 7 8 9 0 81 80 79 78 77

Printed and bound in the United States of America.

Library of Congress Cataloging in Publication Data

Morris, Dean.
  Birds.

  (Read about)
  Includes index.
  SUMMARY: An introduction to various kinds with
emphasis on their behavior in migration, food gathering,
and nest building.
   1. Birds—Juvenile literature. [1. Birds]
I. Title.
QL676.2.M66 598.2 77-8302
ISBN 0-8393-0006-9 lib. bdg.

This book has been reviewed
for accuracy by

Dr. Milton B. Trautman
Professor Emeritus, Curator of Birds
The Ohio State University Museum of Zoology

Don L. Danielson, Director
Schlitz Audubon Center
Milwaukee, Wisconsin

Birds

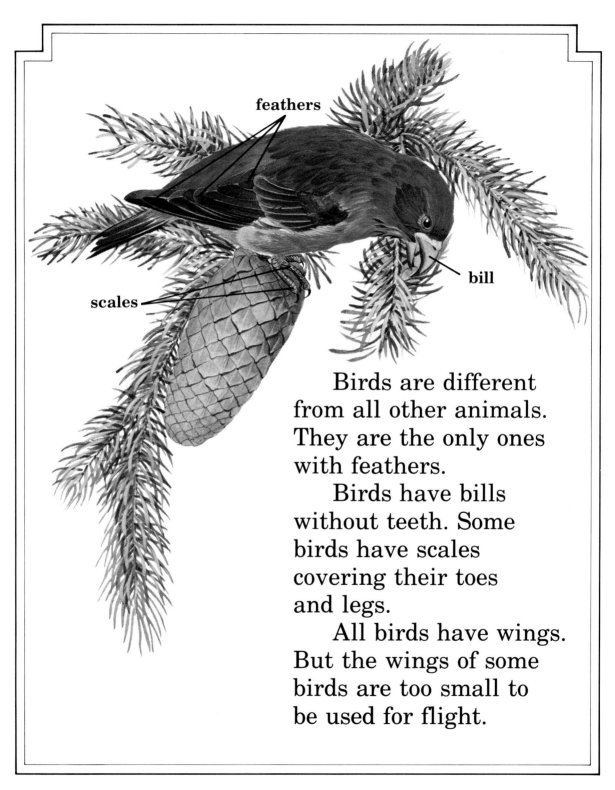

feathers

bill

scales

Birds are different from all other animals. They are the only ones with feathers.

Birds have bills without teeth. Some birds have scales covering their toes and legs.

All birds have wings. But the wings of some birds are too small to be used for flight.

Birds are warm-blooded. That means that a bird's body temperature does not change as the air or water temperature around it changes. Birds can keep warm even when the weather is cold. However, they may freeze to death if the weather becomes too cold.

The wing bones of many birds are hollow and very light. The flight feathers are fastened to them. Primary feathers are fastened to the hand bones. They are the long feathers that propel the bird. Shorter feathers, called secondary feathers, are fastened to the arm bones. They also help keep the bird up in the air.

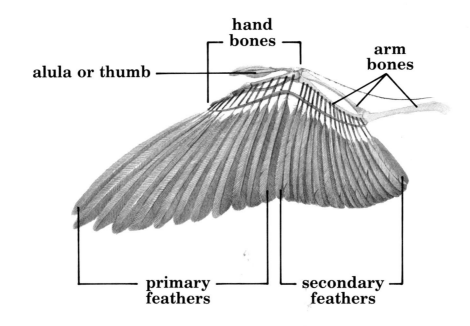

hand
bones

arm
bones

alula or thumb

primary
feathers

secondary
feathers

Each kind of bird needs a special kind of wing shape for the way it lives.

Eagles need very broad wings to lift them high and let them soar slowly to look for food.

Short, rounded wings are for short, quick bursts of speed.

The albatross has very long, narrow wings. They help it glide over the sea.

Penguins cannot fly. They use their wings as flippers to swim underwater.

eagle

albatross

penguin

A bird's wings beat the air when it flies. A bird is able to fly because its feathers close together each time its wings beat down and forward. Air cannot go through the closed feathers. When the bird beats its wings up and backward, the feathers open. Then the air can pass through the wings.

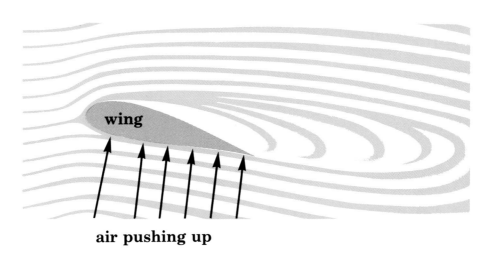

wing

air pushing up

This makes the air move faster over the wing than under the wing. Air pressure builds up under the wings. This helps keep the bird in the air.

The bird's body usually drops a little before the bird beats its wings down again.

The alula feathers on the wings are used the way flaps on the wings of a plane are used.

cardinal

Canada Goose

Golden Eagle

swallow

A bird's bill is made of a hard skin that covers the mouth bones.

Birds use their bills in many ways — to eat, to hold things, and to dig holes.

Birds have bills of different shapes to help them eat different foods. The cardinal has a short, strong bill for cracking seeds. The Canada Goose has a flat bill. It eats plants and insects. The eagle hunts small animals. It has a strong, hooked bill for tearing apart meat and other food. As it flies, the swallow catches insects with its short bill and wide mouth.

Parrots live in tropical regions around the world. Their large bills help them climb trees, eat food, and build nests.

Parrots eat seeds, nuts, and fruit. A parrot can hold food with its feet. It uses its bill to crack nuts and seeds and tear open fruit.

Parrots can make many sounds. They can whistle and make sounds like words.

parrot

toucan

Toucans have curved
bills but short necks.
Their long bills help
them reach out for fruits,
seeds, and other foods.

hummingbirds

Hummingbirds live in North, Central, and South America. They use their long thin bills to get nectar and insects from flowers. These tiny birds can stay in one place in the air by beating their short wings very fast. They can also fly backward.

The Sparrow Hawk, or kestrel, is a bird of prey. Birds of prey hunt other animals for food. They use their strong feet and sharp talons to catch other animals. Some birds of prey, such as owls, hunt for food at night. Hawks, eagles, and vultures hunt in the daytime.

kestrel

Some birds of prey soar slowly, often in circles. It often takes a long time for them to catch animals to eat.

When a bird, such as an Osprey or kestrel, sees its prey, it dives swiftly. After striking its prey, it carries the animal off in its strong feet and sharp talons.

Osprey

The Osprey flies above the water until it sees a fish. Then it drops feet first, grabs the fish with its talons, and flies to a perch to eat the fish.

Woodpeckers use their long, hard bills to hammer into wood, bark, or dead cornstalks for insects and grubs. Woodpeckers often use their feet to hang onto trees and use their tails as props.

Shrikes have strong bills that are hooked at the tip. They often use their strong bills to stick their prey on thorns.

Yellow-bellied Sapsucker

shrike

Swallows and swifts have short bills and wide mouths. They can turn quickly in the air to catch insects. They scoop them up in their mouths as they fly.

Sharp, pointed wings help these birds to fly fast and travel many miles each day.

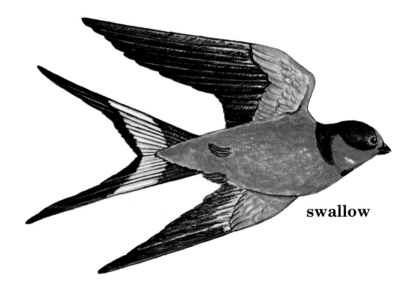

swallow

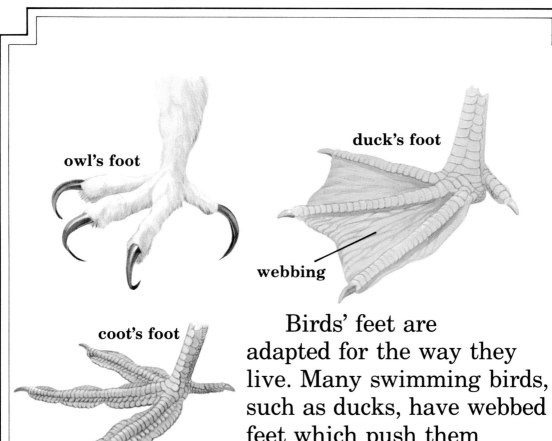

owl's foot

duck's foot

webbing

coot's foot

perching bird's foot

Birds' feet are adapted for the way they live. Many swimming birds, such as ducks, have webbed feet which push them forward in or under the water. Coots are good swimmers too. But their feet are not webbed, they are lobed. Each toe is shaped like a paddle.

Birds of prey, such as owls, have strong feet. Their curved talons can grasp the prey tightly.

Birds that perch have feet that help them hold onto a branch. Usually three toes point forward and one points backward.

Many wading birds, such as herons, have long legs.

The ostrich has long legs too. It cannot fly, but it can run very fast. It has only two strong toes on each foot. The longer toe has a large claw. Ostriches are the largest living birds. The Australian Emu is the second largest bird. It has three strong toes on each foot.

ostrich

Australian Emu

Male and female birds pair up during the mating season.

Birds choose mates in many ways. They sing, dance, boom, strut, drum, or announce their presence in other ways. Some offer gifts.

Grebes are water birds. During the mating season, they shake their heads from side to side. They dance together, too, both in and out of the water.

grebes

The peacock raises its short, stiff, dull-colored tail. The raised tail helps spread the long, beautiful covert feathers. The covert feathers look like a very large fan. The covert feathers are brightly colored. So are the peacock's head and neck.

A male bird sometimes gives a gift to the female. She is called a peahen. The gift may be food, pebbles, or flowers.

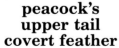

**peacock's
upper tail
covert feather**

peacock

Most birds build a nest each year. The females lay eggs in the nest. Many birds take care of their young until they are old enough to fly. Some birds build nests in trees or bushes. Others lay their eggs on the ground, with or without a nest.

This Song Sparrow's nest is made of grass and sticks. Some nests are lined with wool, hair, and feathers which make them soft. Sparrows often build their nests in a bush or on the ground.

Song Sparrow's nest

The Tailor Bird is named for the way it makes its nest. It sews two leaves together with silk and cobwebs.

Swallows make nests out of mud. They build them on cliffs, on the sides of houses, or on rafters of barns.

The Horned Lark makes its nest on the ground.

Horned Lark's nest

Tailor Bird's nest

swallow's nest

After birds mate the female lays eggs. Most birds sit on the eggs to keep them safe and warm until they hatch. This is called incubation.

Some birds lay their eggs in other birds' nests. There is a cowbird's egg in this Yellow Warbler's nest. The warbler will usually take care of the egg and the young cowbird after it hatches.

The color of most birds' eggs protects them. For example, it is hard for predators to see the Killdeer's eggs.

cowbird's egg

Yellow Warbler's eggs

Killdeer's eggs

Some birds do not build nests. Seabirds often lay their eggs on cliffs or on rocks on the shore.

The guillemot lays its egg on a cliff edge. The egg is shaped like a pear. If it is pushed, it spins around in a circle. It does not often roll off the cliff.

guillemot

egg

swallows

When it gets cold in the north, many birds cannot find food. They fly south to warmer places. When winter is over, they return. This is called migration. However, some birds stay in one area all year.

Some birds fly alone. Others fly in large groups called flocks.

People find out where birds migrate by catching them and putting bands around their legs. Numbers on the bands refer to records which tell where the birds were caught.

The arrows on this map show some of the places where Arctic Terns have been found.

migration pattern of Arctic Terns

shearwaters

Shearwaters are sea-birds that can fly a long way.

At the same time every year, migrating birds return to the same places to lay eggs. Some fly thousands of miles to return to their nesting place.

This map shows where some shearwaters and albatrosses migrate. The Short-tailed Albatross circles the Pacific Ocean from southern Australia to Alaska. The Greater and Manx Shearwaters fly from the south Atlantic Ocean to the north Atlantic and back again.

Birds do not often get lost. We are not sure how they find their way. Some may use the sun, wind, stars, landmarks, or magnetic forces.

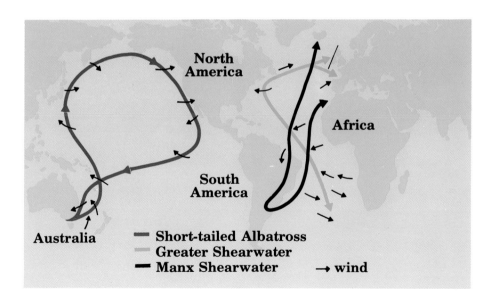

Most birds in the northern hemisphere migrate southward when autumn comes and the days get shorter. Starlings begin to gather in flocks after leaving their nests. Then they fly southward.

Birds sometimes are hurt or get lost when they migrate. Sometimes they get caught in storms as they migrate.

starlings

Some birds travel by day. Perhaps some find their way by looking at the sun.

Some scientists tested this idea. They put starlings in a round cage when it was time to migrate. The cage had many openings for the sun to shine into it.

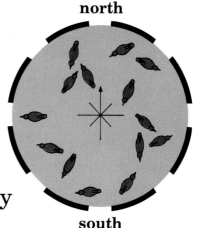

When it was cloudy, the birds perched all around the cage. When the sun was shining, the birds all faced south. This seems to show that birds may use the sun to tell which way to go.

Perhaps birds that travel by night use the stars to guide them.

Homing pigeons are famous for carrying messages. They are very good at finding their way home. People have used them to carry messages for many years.

To train a homing pigeon, a person takes the bird a short way from its home and lets it fly back. Then the person takes it farther away. After the bird returns, it is taken still farther away. Finally it learns to fly home from places hundreds of miles away.

homing pigeons

Rock Doves

Rock Doves, often used for racing, can fly about 45 miles (72 kilometers) an hour.

They may use the sun or landmarks to guide them during the day. Perhaps they get to know the land below them.

Bad weather slows the birds down, but it does not usually stop them.

Where to Read About the Birds

Pronunciation Key for Glossary

a	a as in **cat**, **bad**
ā	a as in **able**, **ai** as in **train**, **ay** as in **play**
ä	a as in **father**, **car**
e	e as in **bend**, **yet**
ē	e as in **me**, **ee** as in **feel**, **ea** as in **beat**, **ie** as in **piece**, **y** as in **heavy**
i	i as in **in**, **pig**
ī	i as in **ice**, **time**, **ie** as in **tie**, **y** as in **my**
o	o as in **top**
ō	o as in **old**, **oa** as in **goat**, **ow** as in **slow**, **oe** as in **toe**
ô	o as in **cloth**, **au** as in **caught**, **aw** as in **paw**, **a** as in **all**
oo	oo as in **good**, **u** as in **put**
oo̅	oo as in **tool**, **ue** as in **blue**
oi	oi as in **oil**, **oy** as in **toy**
ou	ou as in **out**, **ow** as in **plow**
u	u as in **up**, **gun**, **o** as in **other**
ur	ur as in **fur**, **er** as in **person**, **ir** as in **bird**, **or** as in **work**
yo̅o̅	u as in **use**, **ew** as in **few**
ə	a as in **again**, **e** as in **broken**, **i** as in **pencil**, **o** as in **attention**, **u** as in **surprise**
ch	ch as in **such**
ng	ng as in **sing**
sh	sh as in **shell**, **wish**
th	th as in **three**, **bath**
t̲h̲	th as in **that**, **together**

GLOSSARY

These words are defined the way they are used in this book.

adapt (ə dapt′) to change in order to fit new conditions or surroundings

alula (al′ yə lə) a winglike part of a bird's body

announce (ə nouns′) to let something be known

apart (ə pärt′) away from one another

area (er′ ē ə) a certain place or part of something

backward (bak′ wərd) away from; toward the back

bill (bil) the hard part of a bird's mouth

body (bod′ ē) the whole of a person, animal, or plant

bone (bōn) a hard, stiff part of the skeleton of an animal with a backbone

boom (bōōm) to make a deep, hollow sound

broad (brôd) wide from side to side

burst (burst) a sudden breaking out

bush (boosh) a plant with many branches that grows close to the ground

cannot (kan′ ot *or* ka not′) is not able; can not

choose (chōōz) to pick a certain thing or things from among many

claw (klô) a sharp, curved nail on an animal's foot

cobweb (kob′ web′) a network of silk threads spun by a spider

cornstalk (kôrn′ stôk′) the main stem of a corn plant

coverts (kō′ verts) body feathers nearest the upper tail on the lower back of the bird

crack (krak) to break or split something apart

curved (kurvd) bent in one direction

daytime (dā′ tīm′) the time when there is light from the sun

dead (ded) without life; no longer living

death (deth) the end of life for a person, animal, or plant

dive (dīv) to go down through water or air headfirst

drum (drum) to make the sound of something hitting a drum

dull (dul) not interesting; plain

example (eg zam′ pəl) one thing that shows what other things of the same kind are like

fan (fan) a device that looks like part of a circle which can be held and moved back and forth to make a breeze

fasten (fas′ ən) to put things together in a way that they cannot easily come apart

female (fē′ māl) of the sex that has babies or produces eggs

flaps (flaps) give the wings added lift at a reduced speed

flight (flīt) movement through air by using wings; flying

flipper (flip′ ər) a wide, flat limb on a fish or other animal, used for swimming or moving on land

flock (flok) many of the same kind of animals all herded together or gathered together

force (fôrs) to cause something to happen by using great strength

forward (fôr′ wərd) moving ahead

freeze (frēz) to become hard because of the cold

gather (ga<u>th</u>′ ər) to come or bring together in one place

glide (glīd) to float on air

grasp (grasp) to hold onto something firmly

grub (grub) the time of some insects' lives when they look like worms

guide (gīd) to show the way to go or to do something

hammer (ham′ ər) to hit or strike over and over again

hatch (hach) to come from inside an egg

hemisphere (hem′ is fēr′) one-half of the earth divided either from the North Pole to the South Pole or from north and south of the equator

hollow (hol′ ō) having an empty space inside

hooked (hooked) curved

incubation (ing′ kyə bā′ shən) keeping eggs warm by sitting on them until they hatch

insect (in′ sekt) a small animal without a backbone, having a body divided into three parts, three pairs of legs, and usually two pairs of wings

jungle (jung′ gəl) land in warm, damp places covered with many trees, vines, and bushes

kilometer (ki lom′ ə tər *or* kil′ ə mē′ tər) a measure of length that is the same as 3,281 feet

landmark (land′ märk′) a well-known object that stays in place and can be used as a guide

lobed (lōbd) separated into curved, rounded shapes

magnetic (mag net′ ik) with the power to cause iron or steel to move toward it

male (māl) an adult that can father young

map (map) a drawing of part of the surface of the earth, usually showing rivers, oceans, and mountains, and often showing countries and cities

mate (māt) to join in a pair in order to have babies

message (mes′ ij) words that one person or group sends to another person or group

migrate (mī′ grāt) to leave one place and move to another

migration (mī grā′ shən) a movement of a number of living things from one place to another

nectar (nek′ tər) a sweet-tasting liquid formed inside a flower

northern (nor′ thərn) in or toward the north

nut (nut) the dry, shell-covered fruit of
some plants

onto (ôn′ to͞o *or* on′ to͞o) to a place on top
or above

paddle (pad′ əl) a short pole that is wide at
one end, used to move a boat in the water

pear (per) a bell-shaped fruit that grows
on trees

pebble (peb′ əl) a small, rounded, smooth stone

perch (purch) anything a bird can grasp with its
claws and use as a resting place; to sit or rest
on a perch

plane (plān) an aircraft that flies by using
an engine; airplane

predator (pred′ ə tər) an animal that hunts
other animals for food

presence (prez′ əns) being in a certain place
at a certain time

pressure (presh′ ər) the force that results when
one thing pushes against another thing

prey (prā) an animal that another animal hunts
for food

primary (prī′ mer′ ē) the first; the most important

prop (prop) something that is used to hold something else up or keep it in place

propel (prə pel′) to make something move forward

rafter (raf′ tər) a heavy, long piece of wood used to support the roof and floors of a building

record (rek′ ərd) a written story or account of something that tells the facts

refer (ri fur′) to direct a person to a place to get information

region (rē′ jən) a large area

scale (skāl) one of many hard, flat parts that cover the bodies of lizards, fish, and snakes, and parts of some other animals

scientist (sī′ ən tist) someone who has studied a great deal about a branch of science

scoop (skōōp) to take up something with a sweeping motion

season (sē′ zən) a part of the year when a certain thing takes place, such as mating

secondary (sek′ ən der′ ē) the next thing after the first thing; the second in importance

sharp (shärp) having a pointed end that can cut something easily

silk (silk) soft, shiny threads made by some insects

skin (skin) the outer covering of a person's or animal's body

soar (sôr) to fly with only an occasional wing beat

southern (su<u>th</u>′ ərn) in the south; of the south

southward (south′ wərd) toward the south

speed (spēd) fast motion; swiftness

stiff (stif) not able to bend or move easily

storm (stôrm) unusual weather with strong winds, heavy rain or snow, or thunder and lightning

strut (strut) to walk about as if proud of oneself

swift (swift) moving at a fast speed; able to move quickly

talon (tal′ ən) a bird of prey's strong, sharp claw

temperature (tem′ pər ə chər) the amount of heat or coldness

thorn (thôrn) a sharp point that grows on the stem or on a branch of some plants and trees

thousand (thou′ zənd) the number 1,000

travel (trav′ əl) to move from one place to another

tropical (trop′ i kəl) found in the tropics; having to do with the hot regions of the earth

underwater (un′ dər wô′ tər) below the surface of a body of water

wading (wād′ ing) walking in or through water

warm-blooded (wôrm′ blud′ id) having almost the same body temperature all the time

webbed (webd) having the toes of a foot joined by skin growing between them

wool (wool) cloth made from threads spun from the hairs of sheep and some other animals

Bibliography

Allen, Gertrude E. *Everyday Birds.* New York: Houghton Mifflin Company, 1973.

Austin, Elizabeth S. *Birds that Stopped Flying.* New York: Random House, 1968.

Burton, Maurice, and Burton, Robert, editors. *The International Wildlife Encyclopedia.* 20 vols. Milwaukee: Purnell Reference Books, 1970.

Clement, Roland C. *American Birds.* New York: Grosset & Dunlap, 1975.